IMAGES
of America

MISSIONS OF
SAN DIEGO

Sunset Presidio Park... Site of First Cross and First Mission in California

A memorial cross was raised at the 1769 site of Mission San Diego de Alcalá, the first California Spanish mission. The site is where Fr. Junípero Serra dedicated the mission and began the first colony of Alta California claimed by Spanish discovery parties. Established at San Diego's Presidio Park and depicted here in a vintage postcard view, the mission was relocated to its present site in 1774. (Author's collection.)

ON THE COVER: Mission San Diego de Alcalá is pictured in a glass plate from about 1928. Many historic buildings have been restored, recognized, and modernized over many years to preserve all of California's original landmark missions. (Author's collection.)

IMAGES
of America

MISSIONS OF
SAN DIEGO

Robert A. Bellezza

ARCADIA
PUBLISHING

Published by Arcadia Publishing
Charleston, South Carolina

Printed in the United States of America

Library of Congress Control Number: 2013932445

For all general information, please contact Arcadia Publishing:
Telephone 843-853-2070
Fax 843-853-0044
E-mail sales@arcadiapublishing.com
For customer service and orders:
Toll-Free 1-888-313-2665

Visit us on the Internet at www.arcadiapublishing.com

To my daughter, Tara, and her husband, Don Etheridge, who are raising my twin grandsons and choosing fields of educational work in the San Diego area, a mile or so from Mission San Luis Rey de Francia.

CONTENTS

ACKNOWLEDGMENTS

The Library of Congress Prints & Photographs Online Collection has supplied the majority of images within this volume and makes possible a review of California's founding architectural landmarks practically lost through centuries of age, deterioration, and neglect. California's mission buildings were rescued only after the majority had suffered irreversible weathering and ruin to their adobe walls. The Civilian Conservation Corps (CCC) and photographers from the New Deal programs starting in 1933 documented the progress or decay of the many iconic structures through the Historic American Building Survey. Unless otherwise indicated, all images are courtesy of the Library of Congress, Historic American Buildings Survey/Historic American Engineering Record/Historic American Landscapes Survey.

By the beginning of the 20th century, there had been efforts made to preserve the earliest missions, often built and decorated entirely by California natives. Several photographs within this volume are released for the first time from the author's collection and from the Anderson family's collection of vintage glass plates. Many up-to-date mission photographs featured in "Missions Past and Present: Touring El Camino Real" are from the author's visits to each area beginning in 2004.

We are truly pleased our book's release coincides with the 300th anniversary year of Fr. Junípero Serra's birth. Miguel Josep Serra (Junípero was his chosen religious name) was born on November 24, 1713, in Petra, Majorca, one of the Balearic Islands, located some 150 miles off the coast of the Spanish mainland.

INTRODUCTION

The first encampment atop a hill high over San Diego's harbor was established by two land and two sea expeditions and became the first Spanish mission and presidio established in Alta California. A large cross was raised in the sand by Fr. Junípero Serra, Franciscan friar and visionary mission president, who celebrated Mass and the founding of the Mission San Diego de Alcalá on July 16, 1769. Eventually, 21 Spanish missions and their adobe, brick, and stone buildings would grow to productive colonies lasting decades. In recent times, these monumental landmarks of California's heritage have been considered an invaluable part of its history, and all mission buildings have been faithfully restored.

SPANISH GALLEONS AND COLORFUL CONQUISTADORS

The first Spanish settlers adapted the native style of traditional thatched tule reed dwellings on rudimentary earthen floors as the first missions, or they built simple *ramadas*, brush- and mud-encased enclosures. San Diego's aboriginal people—the Kumeyaay, Tipai, and Ipai—were people of white sage and the eagle, who lived for millennia within the diverse microclimatic regions of the Golden State. California native tribes had developed many distinct cultures with unique languages.

In his initial voyage in 1542, Juan Rodriguez Cabrillo anchored the *San Salvador* off Catalina and the islands of the Santa Barbara Channel on his journey to the north, naming Cape Mendocino. In San Diego, Kumeyaay people first responded to Cabrillo by wounding three of his men with arrows. Cabrillo, taking two younger natives aboard, made an effort to communicate with them before releasing the youngsters back on land with new clothing. The message was relayed that he was a peaceful man. Cabrillo had been able to befriend the Chumash, native people of the Channel Islands and Santa Barbara, and they offered food and other provisions to the seafarer.

The official founding of Monterey's harbor in 1602 was consigned to an adventurous Spanish merchant, Don Sebastián Vizcaíno. Carefully charting the entire coast, he claimed possession for Spain, either naming or renaming most ports. The land yet unexplored, Vizcaíno declared Monterey's northern port as ideal and the best possible capital for Alta California. Mexico City, the Spanish capital of the New World, entered a period of prosperity at the time of Vizcaíno's early report but curiously allowed the passage of two centuries before showing interest in exploration to the north.

Privateers and seafaring plunderers under foreign flags had begun to challenge the Spanish holdings, and the voyages made by Capt. James Cook to Tahiti and Hawaii had brought attention to the New World by 1769. Spain had chosen the governor of Baja California, Don Gaspar de Portolá, to muster a first land expedition and venture into Alta California's expansive territories to make permanent Spanish settlements. Joining legendary Fr. Junípero Serra, two mission colonies were planned, one for San Diego and another in Monterey, each following Vizcaíno's earliest descriptions.

The quest for Monterey began after Father Serra founded Mission San Diego de Alcalá in 1769 and a new land expedition had assembled, including friars, an engineer, carpenters, Spanish leather-jacket dragoons, and Baja Indian interpreters followed by a pack train of mules. The overland discovery party passed Santa Monica and Santa Barbara, extending a trail named by the friars El Camino Real, or "The Royal Way," an ancient path blazed by missionaries honoring Carlos I, king of Spain until 1556. Originally, the path reached thousands of miles into the Guatemalan and Mexican jungles, and El Camino Real would now connect Mexico City to Monterey.

Portolá sent search parties out from his campsite near Monterey to discover the features of the coastline, but they were unable to identify Monterey's great harbor. The search ventured into bitterly cold, snowy weather as they attempted to signal from Carmel's shore to a packet lost at sea. With little hope for supplies, the Portolá expedition turned back to the San Diego settlement and the remaining eight colonists, who were also surviving with little food. Portolá ordered plans for the galleon *San Antonio* to return to San Diego's harbor. Despite hardships, a second expedition led by Portolá reached Monterey by land.

Father Serra remained determined to establish his new mission, and the day after Easter in 1770, he boarded the *San Antonio* to embark for Monterey. Father Serra stepped confidently on shore, greeted by Governor Portolá and Fr. Juan Crespí, an early Franciscan chronicler of the overland journeys. The legendary meeting was made at the harbor's edge beneath the Vizcaíno-Serra Oak, which survived hundreds of years after the founding mass of Vizcaíno's party. Consecrating Mission San Carlos de Borromeo on June 3, 1770, to honor King Charles III of Spain, they established the new presidio and capital in Alta California. Jubilant ceremonies and exuberant fanfare were followed by shipboard cannon blasts ringing in concert with the festivities on shore. However, the elation of the settlement was quelled with disturbing news from San Diego of new unrest incited by the first mission neophytes at Mission San Diego de Alcalá. A revolt of nearly 900 mission Indians against the Spanish newcomers led to the loss of several settlers, including Franciscan father Luis Jayme. Previous riots had been stopped after the presidio soldiers defending the settlement killed natives with their muskets. The latest rebellion ignited all the mission buildings with flaming arrows, devastating the settlement. Upon Father Serra's return, Mission San Diego de Alcalá would be separated from the presidio and moved to a new location with a much larger building of adobe, completed in 1780. The present-day Mission San Diego de Alcalá was completed at the site in 1813 and has been restored in modern times using portions of the foundations and remaining walls of the original.

SPAIN'S ERODING POWER

After Monterey's Mission San Carlos de Borromeo was established in 1770, Alta California's mission chain began to spread, with each new mission location about a day's journey from its neighbors. California's modern history would begin during the time of the American Revolution. Thousands had labored to build the new missions, and surrounding colonies commonly were planned as large quadrangles, requiring the regimentation of workers. Hard labor at the missions employed a select number of neophytes working at the sides of master Spanish craftsmen, carpenters, and masons as they constructed the grand stone, adobe brick, and wood buildings. The first changes to the early California landscape, the barren pastures and woodlands now supported self-sustaining communities.

By 1810, many surrounding rancheros had erected small adobe chapels, and integration of church culture was common among the native residents, mission neophytes, the Spanish, and resident Californio vaqueros of Mexico. Mission culture added European-based architecture, music, literature, and art, infusing the succeeding generations with an emerging prosperity in Alta California. The beginning of the Mexican war for independence in 1810 opened a new chapter, bringing the Mexican era to California. A truce ended Spain's dominion over California in 1821, and mission properties were divided or sold under secularized laws favoring local Californios. A major conquest within Alta California shifted to the northern bucolic fields of Sonoma County in 1846.

On June 23, the Bear Flag Revolt, an uprising consisting of 33 Americans from the Sacramento Valley carrying the Bear Flag of the California Republic, encouraged by US Army major John C. Frémont, took possession of the Mission San Francisco de Solano, signaling the end of the Mexican era in California. Mexico's northern commander, Gen. Mariano Guadalupe Vallejo's surrender recognized the new American control of California and sealed the fate of the dated missions and their adobe churches. The Mexican-American War, occurring between 1846 and 1848, resulted in the sleepy province's meteoric ascent to US statehood on September 9, 1850. The mission system had forged the underpinnings of California's first settlements, contributing in unique ways to "how the west was won" nearly a century before the communities of California would be overshadowed by the relentless stampede of immigrants known as the California Gold Rush of 1849.

Mission San Antonio de Pala

Tallied in an 1831 report, livestock in Mission San Luis Rey de Francia's pastures included 26,000 cattle, 25,000 sheep, and over 2,000 horses. The report also noted that the livestock had consumed 395,000 bushels of grain. The settlement counted over 2,000 barrels of mission wine, and its success had piqued the mission's builder, Fr. Antonio Peyri's interest in the eastern regions, which offered tremendous water resources. In nearby agricultural lands, just 20 miles from Mission San Luis Rey de Francia, irrigation water was fed from Warner Springs, native Cupeña land, helping to expand mission boundaries. Father Peyri's founding of the *asistencia* Mission San Antonio de Pala created an important hub to neighboring tribal groups joining the mission communities. A sub-mission at first, Father Peyri had a granary built in 1810; it quickly grew in stature with a mission church and quadrangle of buildings. Beneath the 50-foot bell tower, the sonorous peal of the old mission bells traveled like a beacon throughout the 19th century to bring native faithful within the church. A small chapel was consecrated by 1815, and San Antonio de Pala was deemed a full mission maintained and decorated by faithful Indians. It was crafted from wood timbers and adobe brick and continues today to maintain a tradition of attendance started centuries ago.

Asistencia Santa Ysabel Church

Towards the edge of the eastern desert, Mission San Diego de Alcalá's trails led to an asistencia requested by Fr. Juan Mariner, and the inaugural Mass was celebrated in September 1818. It eventually became a critical destination. Named Mission Santa Ysabel to honor Elizabeth of Portugal (born in 1271), the location was just 35 miles from downtown San Diego, near the mining town of Julian. The mission chapel was built at a 3,000 foot elevation and featured a granary, several adobes, and a cemetery. It served hundreds of Luiseño and Diegueño Indians from the nearby foothills and mountains east of San Diego.

The Mission Santa Ysabel church bells were raised on a wooden scaffold near an adobe mission building for many years. The bells were perhaps the oldest of the entire mission chain, brought by early mission Indians who carried them by mule from San Diego. They disappeared after 1913, and only the bell clappers were found; a museum was set up at the mission site soon after. The mystery of their loss has continued after the first mission vanished into the soil long before. In 1924, a new Church of St. John the Baptist was erected at the site of the original Mission Santa Ysabel asistencia, and it remains today.

Missions Past and Present

California's founding landmarks and their hallowed adobe halls have been revered by visitors for centuries. The 21 California mission buildings were built in magnificent scale, proportion, and grand design to each reflect an individual beauty blending Spanish, Moorish, and Mexican architecture with highlights of decorative designs and carvings often created by early mission

Indians using mixtures of soft and glowing natural colors. Travelers have often compared the value of their historical significance to visiting the iconic pyramids of Egypt. Centuries of wet weather and earthquakes affected the venerable buildings, irreversibly deteriorating to piles of earthen rubble. The friars had been forced to flee intolerant living conditions, and many were given passage to return to their homelands. The neophyte converts sadly dispersed at the loss of the mission colonies, further complicated by severe epidemics devastating two-thirds of their population. Mission Indians often lost their native traditions after generations of indoctrination. The old landmarks would dissolve into their foundations or remain partially standing by the 20th century. Only a few missions had been kept serviceable, and each had been the victim of earthquakes and fires.

All of the missions have been rebuilt and received accurate restorations in the recent years. A bygone era of Old California's romantic landscape has been revitalized. The restoration process began in 1888 with the Association for the Preservation of the Missions; by 1895, it had carried over to the Landmarks Club, headed by Charles Fletcher Lummis, an influential newspaper writer. The club leased Mission San Juan Capistrano, rescuing it from utter ruin, and made efforts at rebuilding Mission San Fernando in 1899, Mission San Diego de Alcalá, and Mission San Antonio de Pala. A beloved Franciscan father, Joseph Jeremiah O'Keefe, originally from Ireland, became a major restorer of southern missions after decades of effort at Mission San Luis Rey de Francia. The Historic Landmarks League in 1902, Native Sons and Native Daughters of the Golden West, California State Parks, the Hearst Foundation, the Franciscan Order and Catholic Church, and several US presidents have added to community efforts to preserve these remarkable pieces of California's esteemed history.

One

THE 1769 EXPEDITION
MISSION SAN DIEGO DE ALCALÁ

Depicted in the timeless beauty of this late 19th century photograph, California's first mission was named for Saint Didacus of Alcalá in 1769. Mission San Diego de Alcalá was moved from the presidio by 1774 and rebuilt with adobe bricks at the new site. The present iconic building was completed by 1813. Over many years the mission served multiple uses, and was eventually completely neglected.

This southern view was taken above the valley from Mission San Diego de Alcalá's first location. Capt. Fernando Xavier de Rivera y Moncada, military governor of Alta California from 1773 to 1777, had scouted the first trails nearly three weeks before Don Gaspar de Portolá, the governor of Baja California, led the first founding party of 75 men. Forty Christian Indian men from Baja accompanied Portolá and Rivera to begin San Diego's first settlement.

The simple native hut, or *kish*, is documented at a native Cahuilla home outside Palm Desert in an image taken in 1924 by Edward S. Curtis, a renowned photographer portraying America's Indians at a pivotal turn-of-the-century period. The convergence of natives and soldiers caused friction at the first mission settlements. An upheaval came from within the mission and erupted into conflicts in which the first settlement in San Diego was burned down.

San Diego's Presidio Hill is seen here looking eastward towards the second Mission San Diego de Alcalá site in 1936. The rural landscape is largely unchanged from pioneer days and represents how the land may have looked before it was explored. Spanish packets had come to the San Diego harbor from Mexico's seaport at San Blas. Supplies would be carried by mule trains to furnish the outer settlements along El Camino Real.

A rare treasure created in 1787, this is the frontispiece from the diary of Fr. Francisco Palóu, a close companion and main biographer of the pioneer missionary Fr. Junípero Serra during the earliest settlements. Father Palóu's writings were published as the *Life of Serra*, a diary written during Alta California's discovery days. The padres traveled together from Mexico City's Franciscan College of San Fernando and were sent under the agreement of Spain's visitor general. A plan to implement Alta California's first settlements included a widespread system of missions, asistencias, and *estancias* throughout California. The mission succeeded, planting roots and settling many familiar California towns.

V. R. DEL V. P. F. JUNIPERO SERRA

In 1774, Father Serra moved the mission to a site six miles from the presidio near the fertile San Diego River bank. After surviving as ruins for over a century, the 1813 church was restored and rededicated in 1931. Mission San Diego de Alcalá's remaining freestanding facade was sadly left to decay. The rear of the church and adobe monastery walls and portico were in ruins. After the buildings had been restored and the *campanario* reconstructed, an innovative live radio simulcast was created for thousands to hear the public ceremonies broadcast from the mission.

The remaining bell at Mission San Diego de Alcalá stood at a revered spot on the ruins of the ancient mission campanile. By the beginning of the 20th century, new attention was paid by preservationists to the mission's ruined condition, with most rear portions of the adobe buildings missing or carried away to other buildings. The mission property had been returned to the Catholic Church in 1862. (Southwest Museum of the American Indian Collection.)

On Sunday, September 13, 1931, a Pontifical High Mass was held within Mission San Diego de Alcalá as part of a two-day celebration rededicating the 162-year-old mission church. The mission had been founded by Fr. Junípero Serra as a simple brushwood ramada and relocated to its present site in 1774 before being struck down by earthquakes in 1803 and 1812. This photograph, from around 1930, was taken near the completion of the first restoration.

A vintage postcard commemorates the first arrival to Alta California's rugged coastline by Juan Rodriguez Cabrillo, a Portuguese navigator anchoring off Catalina Island in 1542. He landed in San Diego and named the port San Miguel, later exploring the Santa Barbara Channel and north, where he discovered and named Cape Mendocino. Cabrillo's legacy claimed California for the Spanish crown and included charting many important harbors and presidio sites. In a stroke of ill fate, he unexpectedly died from a broken arm. He was buried on San Miguel Island in the Santa Barbara Channel. Fr. Junípero Serra and the first settlement arrived over two centuries later in 1769. The Cabrillo National Monument is located in San Diego at land's end off Catalina Boulevard on Point Loma. The silhouetted sculpture represents Cabrillo's caravel-style ship, the *San Salvador*. (Author's collection.)

This Diegueño home was photographed by Edward S. Curtis in 1924. *Diegueño* was a name designated by the padres to broadly identify all natives living near Mission San Diego de Alcalá. As in all of California, diversified groups had adapted to their habitats throughout San Diego County and developed distinct dialects.

California's Mission San Diego de Alcalá has stood for over two centuries. An early expedition of Hernando Cortéz sent explorers to Mexico's northern coast, and in 1539, Francisco de Ulloa sailed the entire coast of the Vermillion Sea, or Sea of Cortez, to determine that Baja California was a peninsula and that the fabled northern passage, the Straits of Anián, did not exist. (Southwest Museum of the American Indian Collection.)

A turn-of-the-century photograph from a lantern slide by the Beseler Company shows the mission prior to the Landmarks Club's restoration of 1899. Sadly neglected, Mission San Diego de Alcalá presented an important precedent for preserving the founding landmarks of California. (Author's collection.)

The earliest mission had become a US Army depot, a Mission Indian school, and a native settlement after steady deterioration when the building was abandoned. Only the facade and rear adobe walls were left standing by 1899.

In a 1915 Keystone View Company stereograph slide, Mission San Diego de Alcalá appeared an idle curiosity or relic. During the mission's prime years, the monastery was fully developed into a large quadrangle. It consisted of shops, residences, and storage with a patio in a square of 120 feet. Due to deterioration over the years, only a small part of the monastery was preserved.

The Mission San Diego de Alcalá's massive 1,200-pound bell, *Mater Dolorosa*, had been recast in 1894 from five original bells at the mission cast in San Diego in 1796. (Southwest Museum of the American Indian Collection.)

The portico at Mission San Diego de Alcalá is pictured here. The missionaries marched to the north, founding 21 missions along El Camino Real and connecting unexplored territories with the new Spanish colonies of California. (Escondido Public Library, Pioneer Room.)

Artifacts of Spanish origin left by the earliest settlers have been unearthed over many archeological digs in and around the first site. The settlement at Mission San Diego de Alcalá had little significance to the native Indians at first; they were uninterested except when offered provisions in trade. They reportedly loved to possess cloth to the point of raiding ships, and sailcloth became highly desirable. (Southwest Museum of the American Indian Collection.)

A vintage postcard of old Mission San Diego de Alcalá depicts the ruins as seen by the public in the early 1900s, a reminder of the earliest history of romantic Spanish California. The Spanish missions were at the heart of civilization in early California and would last for 54 years, predating the Gold Rush of 1849. (Escondido Public Library, Pioneer Room.)

In 1780, a new adobe church was built on today's location and completed with walls three feet thick as part of a quadrangle. A new and much larger church was begun in 1808 and completed in 1813 on November 12, the feast day honoring patron saint Didacus. (Author's collection.)

This photograph taken after full restoration shows the Mission San Diego de Alcalá about 1951. It was taken by Eloise Perkins, an Escondido newspaper photographer who documented the surrounding San Diego County history. (Escondido Public Library, Pioneer Room.)

In a 1905 photograph, the old adobe brick pedestal still holds the surviving bell of Mission San Diego de Alcalá. The belfry had been a symbolic part of the traditional missions, and here it is in ruins left for mission restorers. The mission was lovingly restored by 1931. (Southwest Museum of the American Indian Collection.)

Treasures from the 15th century, like an *escritorio*, or writing desk, depicted in this souvenir postcard, were brought from Europe by the Spanish friars and now reside within the Serra Museum collection near Old San Diego. (Author's collection.)

This stained-glass window design is from the Library of Congress collection devoted to Mission San Diego de Alcalá. The church, belfry, a neophyte, and a garden tended by Father Serra are shown along with the text "Fr Junipero Serra, AD. 1769."

This photograph from around 1945 shows a visitor posed at the front entrance of Mission San Diego de Alcalá. The San Diego mission was at the beginning of California's El Camino Real, leading early missionaries as far as 650 miles north and reaching to Sonoma's Mission San Francisco Solano. (Author's collection.)

A photograph taken at Mission San Diego de Alcalá in 1956 reveals the restored mission, which has fully recaptured its former luster, surrounded by lush, mature gardens. Today, the mission may be visited a few miles off Interstate 5, Friars Way, on San Diego Mission Road. (Escondido Library Pioneer Room.)

A rear perspective shows the east facade at the restored Mission San Diego de Alcalá. The walls had been made from adobe, but burned brick was used as a main material for pilasters, moldings, the belfry, the dome over the mortuary chapel, the altars, and the arches, which were all finished with plaster.

This Historical American Building Survey photograph from 1936 documents the restoration, featuring the massive wooden entry door at the south wall at Mission San Diego de Alcalá.

A photograph from the late 1800s shows Mission San Diego de Alcalá after the US Army had camped there following the Mexican-American War. The Army had appreciated the sweeping view of the valley of the San Diego River, as well as the three-foot-thick walls defending them from attackers.

The friar's chair used by Father Serra was carved by Spanish craftsmen. Father Serra traveled to Monterey bringing several liturgical treasures, including a folded silver traveling altar. He presided as California mission president from his headquarters at Mission San Carlos Borromeo del Rio Carmelo until 1784. (Southwest Museum of the American Indian Collection.)

This view from the church balcony was taken for the Historic American Building Survey of 1937. The church nave at Mission San Diego de Alcalá displays decorative plaster frescos of native patterns with soft colors from the 1931 recreation. The survey noted that the mission's foundations were of "field stone and the old front wall appears to be brick and buttresses and front are of stone, brick faced and plastered," and its interior had been observed with "walls restored of adobe brick, stone and concrete, plastered inside and out, wood framed balcony and roof, tile floor and roofing. Walls are white washed." The Spanish missions created a large footprint both historically and physically.

Spanish artifacts discovered in 1869 and 1871 included swords among the rare treasures left from earliest residents. The first revolt within Mission San Diego de Alcalá left several dead, including the head missionary, Fr. Luis Jayme. It was later found to be the work of two rebellious mission Indians. Governor Rivera followed one miscreant into the church sanctuary, and Rivera, brandishing a sword within the church, led the submissive man into guardhouse stocks. Rivera was excommunicated immediately over the incident, but it was the last of the San Diego mission rebellions. (Southwest Museum of the American Indian Collection.)

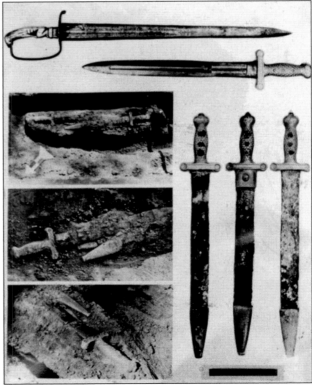

This c. 1890 photograph captures a former governor, Don Antonio Coronel, next to the first Spanish cannon brought to the territory, depicting the romantic side of California's turbulent past. At the side of Fr. Junípero Serra, leatherjackets at the presidios had carried Spanish cannons for authority and defense, and fired them during celebrations of their triumphs. The Spanish founded four presidio settlements in Alta California. (Southwest Museum of the American Indian Collection.)

An excavated cellar stair at the first settlement is exposed by modern archeologists in 1971. Modern safety reinforcements were added in later years, and all mission buildings have been restored using early materials with modern techniques. (Southwest Museum of the American Indian Collection.)

Mission San Diego de Alcalá became a highly regarded attraction for visitors, and the authentic restoration encourages historians, photographers, and artists today. Little remained of the original rear walls of the church; only the facade stood firmly as a reminder of the original 1813 building. (Southwest Museum of the American Indian Collection.)

Serene surroundings imbue the mission adobe walls with a nostalgic and romantic mystique. Absent of its campanario, the mission remained abandoned until the late-19th-century Landmarks Club began preservation efforts, headed by Charles F. Lummis, its president. (Southwest Museum of the American Indian Collection.)

Mission Indian baskets were used often at old Mission San Diego de Alcalá, as portrayed in a rare 1892 photograph at the front entry. The native denizens in this early photograph are Diegueños, a name describing the local Indians in the region of the old mission. (Escondido Public Library, Pioneer Room.)

Continuing excavations are made for archeology as in 1971 at the original settlement of the first Mission San Diego de Alcalá at the San Diego presidio site. A subterranean cellar was exposed that is thought to be a storeroom. (Southwest Museum of the American Indian Collection.)

An early burial site at Mission San Diego de Alcalá's first presidio was uncovered in 1971. Archeologists paid attention to clues of cultural lifestyles and influences of the earliest explorers, matching this with the chronicles from the era. The San Diego History Center is located at the museum atop Presidio Hill at the original settlement site of Alta California. (Southwest Museum of the American Indian Collection.)

J.D. Spreckels, the great sugar magnate, was aware of the potential for a Mission Cliff Park, although it consisted only of seven palm trees and a large pavilion overlooking Mission Valley. In 1902, he hired a Scottish gardener, John Davidson, to take care of the few trees and flowers and began Mission Cliff Gardens. The gardens were closed to the public in 1929 and today lie within a modern subdivision. (Author's collection.)

San Diego's Cahuilla tribe preserved their language for modern times, as several chants and traditional dances of the Southwest Indians were recorded and often released on 78 r.p.m. records by RCA Victor in the 1920s. Oral traditions had been historically passed through generations to document the many surviving stories from the mission era. (Southwest Museum of the American Indian Collection.)

BELL TOWER, MISSION SAN DIEGO DE ALCALA.
SAN DIEGO, CALIFORNIA—86

A Midwestern newspaperman, Charles Fletcher Lummis walked his way to Los Angeles sending back reports of the West. He was responsible for forming the California Landmarks Club in 1895, rescuing the Mother Mission, the Serra Cross, and El Camino Real, and doing important work in the preservation and restoration of the missions of San Fernando, San Juan Capistrano, San Luis Rey, San Diego, and the Pala asistencia. (Author's collection.)

After Mission San Diego de Alcalá was restored and its lush gardens fully grown, the pierced *espanada* tower with its five suspended mission bells was often depicted in vintage postcards. Relocating in 1774, a new mission structure built in 1780 measured 84 feet by 15 feet with adobe walls three feet thick. Its buildings, set in a quadrangle, included the church and monastery. To the rear, a wall led to a tannery tank for hides, sheep corrals, and a cow barn. The first tile roof came in 1793, and a large granary was constructed there. The present mission church and quadrangle were reconstructed after the earthquake of 1812. (Author's collection.)

Generations of mission Indians had lived in San Diego's downtown, and by 1888, Father Antonio Ubach learned that his contract for housing 75 pupils had been renewed. City officials encouraged Father Ubach to transfer the school to Mission San Diego de Alcalá's abandoned site. The *San Diego Union* reported on Father Ubach's plans "to remove the St. Anthony Indian school from Old Town to the more expansive grounds of the Mission farm, six miles up the valley, a century ago filled with the rancherias of these children's ancestors." (Southwest Museum of the American Indian Collection.)

The patio garden and inner court of Mission San Diego de Alcalá are displayed in this vintage postcard. The rate of conversions of mission neophytes was one of the most successful of all 21 missions in Alta California. (Author's collection.)

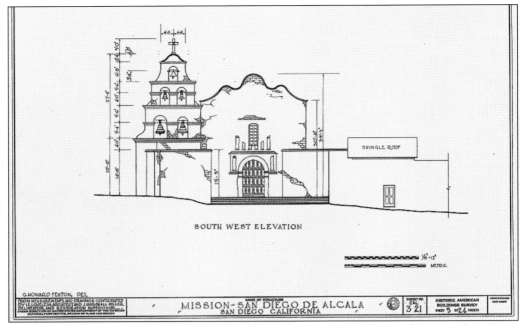

A historic US survey of the late 1930s carefully archived the condition of Mission San Diego after restoration. Henry F. Withey, photographer for the WPA, included general descriptions of several buildings.

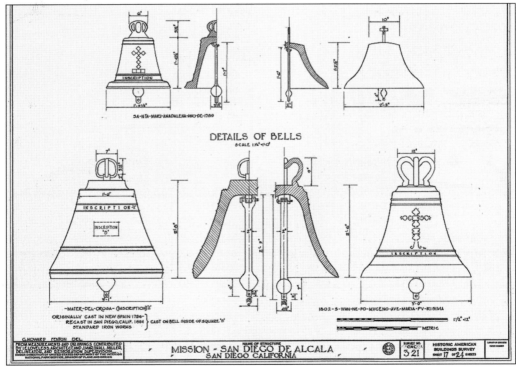

The inscriptions on the bells read: "SA-NTA-MARI-AHADALEHA-ANO-DE-1789," MATER-DEL-OROSA," "Originally cast in New Spain 1796–Recast in San Diego, Calif. 1894, Standard Iron Works," and "1802-S-IVAN-NE-PO-MVCENO-AVE-MARIA-PV-RISIMA."

36

Two

THE "KING OF THE MISSIONS"
MISSION SAN LUIS REY DE FRANCIA

The "King of the Missions" was fully restored by 1937, and old Mission San Luis Rey de Francia presents a commanding footprint even by today's standards. In 1793, Oceanside became the ideal location for Fr. Fermín de Lasuén to establish the 18th Alta California mission. Mission San Luis Rey de Francia's impressive Moorish-influenced design merged cleanly in the secluded San Luis Rey River Valley. Four miles inland from the Pacific Ocean, the site offered cool, dry weather and perfect terrain to sustain abundant agricultural enterprise. (Author's collection.)

The King of the Missions is pictured in 1937. Mission San Luis Rey de Francia was the last of nine missions Fr. Fermín Francisco de Lasuén founded as mission president. The mission site had been planned for Mission San Juan Capistrano but was moved farther north at an earlier date. The site closed the gap between the first mission in San Diego and those along El Camino Real in the north. (Anderson family collection.)

The baptismal font and ritual are the symbolic entry to life within the church. Mission San Luis Rey de Francia's original piece was of hand-hammered copper made by mission Indians and was located inside a niche to the left of the front door. Father Lasuén baptized 54 children the day of the mission's founding in 1798, and by 1815, the mission had become the largest and most prosperous in California's chain of 21. (Southwest Museum of the American Indian Collection.)

San Diego's diversified geography contained small ranchos and had supported several estancia chapels served by visiting padres. Old El Camino Real in Oceanside connected Mission San Luis Rey de Francia and the very first, Mission San Diego de Alcalá, to the south. Historical signage with bell markers created at the beginning of the 20th century guide motorists on El Camino Real to mission landmarks throughout the state. (Anderson family collection.)

San Luis Rey (King Louis IX in 13th-century France) was a lay affiliate of the Franciscan order and is represented by a revered sculpture within the arched niche over the entrance to the mission church. A full-size statue of Saint Louis is kept within Mission San Luis de Francia near the church entry. (Southwest Museum of the American Indian Collection.)

Visiting on the feast of Saint Anthony de Padua during the mission anniversary celebration in 1827, a Frenchman, Captain Duhaut-Cilly, wrote of a feast begun with religious services and chanting and music for High Mass given entirely by neophyte Indians, who had made their own hand-carved instruments. At the conclusion, the church services were followed by a bullfight performed by skilled horsemen and an exhausted steer, tossing it to the ground by the tail from horseback.

Father O'Keefe, at left, was the earliest mission restorer at Mission San Luis Rey de Francia in 1892. He began restorations by excavating the *lavandero* site and stairs as well as making major repairs to the church. New quarters and dormitories were erected in 1898, taking the place of structures fallen in ruins during the last half of the 19th century. He returned to Santa Barbara in 1912, and Fr. Peter Wallischeck continued his efforts. Retrofitting required rebuilding the church roof during 2013 for earthquake safety. (Southwest Museum of the American Indian Collection.)

A rare photograph shows the church rededication of May 13, 1893. Fr. Joseph Jeremiah O'Keefe had been directed to set up the Franciscan missionary college in Oceanside at Mission San Luis Rey de Francia, and he continued over 19 years to oversee much of the early restoration. (Southwest Museum of the American Indian Collection.)

A conference of novitiates is held in 1900 at the Mission San Luis Rey de Francia. The Franciscan Order has continued to lead the mission restoration into modern times. (Southwest Museum of the American Indian Collection.)

Above the crested archway of the church facade stands a cement cross directly above the entry doors. The view from the mission rooftop looking west reveals the open landscape of the San Luis Rey River Valley and the mission property, which once covered a 15-mile radius to the sea's edge.

At the top of the campanile, the view shows the eastern church dome over a copper-sheathed octagonal cupola and lantern. The lantern holds 144 panes of glass and allows light within the church's interior. The massive church transepts extend on each side in a cruciform shape, adding extra room for attendees. Additions were made to the rear of the sacristy and oratory buildings in 1832.

The *presidente* of Los Caballeros del Camino Real is pictured astride his palomino in celebration of the 171st birthday of Old Mission San Luis Rey de Francia in 1964. The commemoration of events and festivals is part of the California mission culture and joins many communities' diverse populations to the oldest historical sites throughout the state. (Escondido Public Library, Pioneer Room.)

Looking at the north facade of Mission San Luis Rey de Francia's mortuary chapel, a side extension projects into the nave with an unusual balcony area made for viewing the altar and ceremonies for the deceased. The interior of the elaborate mortuary chapel is built in an octagonal shape and includes its own private altar.

Franciscan padres had left their notations, diaries, and resource books containing many early European designs and ideas for building the elaborate California missions. The friendliness of many natives to the early padres had accelerated the program at Mission San Luis Rey de Francia of building the mission site. Over 8,000 bricks were produced to begin construction of the church, and soldiers from the San Diego presidio were required to participate to complete the settlement. (Southwest Museum of the American Indian Collection.)

Many artifacts are given special displays at the mission, including a large revolving music stand and several illuminated-manuscript singing books. After the effect of Mexican laws by 1832, Fr. Antonio Peyri was no longer able to keep discipline at the mission, and one night he left with two aspiring neophytes, Pablo Tac and Agapito Amamix, to San Diego, where the ship *Pocahontas* had been waiting. His departure was so grieved that the remaining mission Indians followed him the next day by swimming towards the departing galleon as it left the port. (Southwest Museum of the American Indian Collection.)

Mission San Luis de Francia honors King Louis IX of France, an affiliate of the Franciscan Order who lived between 1215 and 1270. The mission was abandoned between 1865 and 1892, then rededicated in 1893, and is historically the largest California mission. A second tower had been designed but never built during the time of construction by Fr. Antonio Peyri.

L.C. Settle of Los Caballeros del Camino Real rides the Royal Way during a historic annual fiesta at Old Mission San Luis Rey de Francia in July in the 1960s. Since 1937, the buildings and gardens have been continuously restored and open to the public for visits, retreats, and festivities. (Escondido Public Library, Pioneer Room.)

Nearly 180 feet in length, the mission church was richly decorated by the Luiseño Mission Indians in rich colors. At left in the photograph above, the old Byzantine pulpit has no canopy or sounding board. To each side of the main altar are the extended winged transepts from the center nave, enough room for nearly 1,000 in attendance. (Southwest Museum of the American Indian Collection.)

The side altar within the transept is pictured in a photograph facing west inside Mission San Luis Rey de Francia. In 1811, the present church foundations were laid by Fr. Antonio Peyri for his grandest of mission churches and towering campanario. The native population by 1810 had increased to more than 1,500 from the original 432 neophytes. The completed church was dedicated on the feast of Saint Francis, October 4, 1815.

Father Lasuén founded the mission in 1798, and construction of the mission and quadrangle was carried out by Father Peyri in 1811. Over the next century, the church lay in ruins until the humble remains were brought back to their full grandeur by the ardent efforts of Father O'Keefe, who rededicated the church in 1893. As details were added by 1937, restorations to the interior art were made by skilled artisans through the American Index of Design, a product of the New Deal era. (Escondido Public Library, Pioneer Room.)

Mission San Luis Rey de Francia's magnificent chapel nave accommodated up to 1,000 attendees within its hallowed walls. The massive church may be entered at the scalloped door opening leading through the three-foot adobe walls of the church to an inner courtyard.

The remaining quadrangular archways frame a patio square measuring 500 feet in each direction. The cloisters were filled once with flowers and shrubs gracing the surroundings of the imposing mission structure. (Southwest Museum of the American Indian Collection.)

Mission San Luis Rey de Francia stands nearly restored in a photograph from 1937. Between 1798 and 1832 the mission recorded 5,397 baptisms, 1,335 marriages, and 2,716 deaths. The mission grew in size to cover six acres of cloistered resident buildings within its quadrangle, and the grand church was the largest of all 21 California missions. (Anderson family collection.)

The first day of the founding of Mission San Luis Rey de Francia was witnessed by a great multitude of native inhabitants, and 54 neophytes were baptized. During the first month of the mission, over 8,000 adobe bricks were manufactured and the building foundations laid. (Escondido Public Library, Pioneer Room.)

Mission San Luis Rey de Francia's tiered belfry and Spanish-influenced Moorish design, created by Fr. Antonio Peyri (pictured here) was considered a masterpiece of architectural simplicity. In 1926, the massive tower structure succumbed to heavy rains and earlier earthquake damage, causing its collapse. It was rebuilt in 1927. The architectural influence has carried through centuries and been repeated in Mission Revival designs. (Southwest Museum of the American Indian Collection.)

Only the church and a few walls of archways of the original Mission San Luis Rey de Francia remained at the beginning of the 20th century. The Carriage Arch stands today, the original entrance to the inner buildings of the mission. The view through the arch reveals the oldest pepper tree planted in California at the mission garden.

There were originally 36 archways, but unrelenting erosion ultimately decimated many old adobe structures over six acres of grounds. The Mormon Battalion and other US troops had quartered at Mission San Luis Rey de Francia, which was later abandoned for many years, during the Mexican-American War. (Escondido Public Library, Pioneer Room.)

In August 1846, US lieutenant colonel John C. Frémont assigned John Bidwell to secure the mission and surrounding region. In December 1846, Kit Carson and Col. Stephen Kearney camped at Mission San Luis Rey, and by January 2, 1847, Colonel Kearny's weary US troops arrived at the mission to defend the United States during the Mexican-American War. Mexico ceded California to the United States by signing the Treaty of Guadalupe Hidalgo in February 1848 and the treaty was ratified in Congress on March 10, 1848.

At 79 years of age, Fr. Fermín Francisco de Lasuén established Mission San Luis Rey de Francia as his last, celebrating its founding on June 13, 1798, in a small mud-covered ramada by conducting baptisms of 54 neophytes. The ceremony took place on the feast day of Saint Anthony of Padua. Attendees included Fr. Antonio Peyri, the mission's first guardian, as well as Spanish soldiers and members of the San Luis Rey band of Luiseño Mission Indians. (Southwest Museum of the American Indian Collection.)

The Franciscan friars regarded historic preservation of native artifacts important at the dawn of the 20th century. Fr. Joseph Jeremiah O'Keefe had rediscovered early structures left by neophytes and the first padres, including an extensive burned-brick-lined *lavanderia* fed by two springs through two gargoyle-shaped outlets just below the mission quadrangle. (Southwest Museum of the American Indian Collection.)

The archways surrounding the courtyard are still visible around 1890 and reveal the unending erosion at the grand King of the Missions. El Camino Real brought early motorists to these magnificent ruins to spend the day. Visitors often included writers, artists, photographers, and archeologists who documented the historic landmark. (Escondido Public Library, Pioneer Room.)

Early restorations included rebuilding the gardens that included California's oldest pepper tree within the mission's courtyard. The tree was planted by Fr. Antonio Peyri from a seedling brought by ship nearly two centuries ago. (Escondido Public Library, Pioneer Room.)

By 1810, the native population had increased to more than 1,500 from the original 432 neophytes. The mission had four *rancherios* or settlements with estancia chapels. They included San Juan, Santa Margarita, San Jacinto, and Las Flores. An asistencia, San Antonio de Pala, was established in June 1816 about 20 miles east. (Escondido Public Library, Pioneer Room.)

This gate led to the lavanderia, with it sunken gardens and staircase; two springs flowed over the brick-lined floor. In 1937, the site had been thoroughly cleared. It was rebuilt by the 1960s and can be visited today at the front of the mission.

In 1958, reconstruction revealed an elaborate system of waterways feeding the lavanderia that included a charcoal water filter. The sunken garden area at the front of Mission San Luis Rey de Francia had clay pipes with water fed throughout the six-acre mission quadrangle that had been developed from the earliest days. (Southwest Museum of the American Indian Collection.)

Restoration work took place in 1958 at the sunken garden lavanderia and soldiers' barracks. Each was excavated and rebuilt. (Southwest Museum of the American Indian Collection.)

A view of the main Mission San Luis Rey altar shows the iconic Our Lady of Guadalupe at the center. Fr. Joseph Jeremiah O'Keefe spent 1893 to 1912 repairing the church interior and roof. All exposed beams had been covered, and seating had been set forward to accommodate attendees. The original altar *reredos* exhibits a Baroque-influenced flare, common at many California missions. (Southwest Museum of the American Indian Collection.)

Mission San Luis Rey de Francia's church entry at the nave is shown in the 1930s. After the reconstruction and restoration, the mission housed a Franciscan college that ended after a few decades. Today, the mission offers retreats, and its grounds are a destination often visited by tourists, pilgrims, and the faithful of the area.

Fr. Joseph Jeremiah O'Keefe led reconstruction and restorations, photographed at the staircase and the private garden built by Fr. Antonio Peyri, the mission's architect and builder. The mission's preservation continued under Father O'Keefe through 1912, when permanent quarters were completed and the quadrangle was scaled to about one-fourth the original size. (Southwest Museum of the American Indian Collection.)

A photograph made for a vintage postcard in the late 1930s reveals the grandest of all California missions, Mission San Luis de Rey de Francia. The rededication of Mission San Luis Rey de Francia came in 1893, and refugees of the Franciscan Zacatecas Order from Mexico fleeing political hardships had moved there. After 1912, Fr. Peter Wallischeck carried out many restorations to bring the mission back to the improved condition seen today. (Author's collection.)

Mission San Luis Rey de Francia had been returned to the church from Mexican secularization to avoid further plundering of the property in 1843 by Gov. Manuel Micheltorena. Pres. Abraham Lincoln emancipated the church by returning many of the California missions' title patents back to church ownership in 1865 in a proclamation just weeks before his assassination. (Author's collection.)

The garden cemetery and grounds flourished at Mission San Luis Rey de Francia with a system of abundant water supplying over six acres. A view taken in the early 1950s includes the oldest California pepper tree, brought from Peru about 1830 and planted by Father Peyri, the mission's builder and architect. (Escondido Public Library, Pioneer Room.)

Portrayed in vintage mission postcards, the portico and entry at Mission San Luis Rey de Francia, the King of Missions, displays what remains of its former majestic condition. Of the original 32 brick arches surrounding the courtyard, 12 were rebuilt during the modern restoration. (Author's collection.)

Mission San Luis Rey de Francia displays a massive two-tiered bell tower and church facade defined by Moorish lines along its high pediment and entablature, with a small round window at the center above decorative pilasters at the sides of the doorway entrance.

The millstone meant great productivity at all missions. The successful neighbors helped the newly founded mission in 1798, sending Mission San Luis Rey de Francia horses, oxen, cattle, and sheep from the surrounding missions Santa Barbara, San Juan Capistrano, San Gabriel, and San Diego. (Southwest Museum of the American Indian Collection.)

The expansive grounds of Mission San Luis Rey de Francia included an archway to a sunken garden area where a large brick-lined lavanderia used to wash clothes and bathe was fed by two springs. The mission drinking water was filtered through charcoal, and a limekiln was built nearby for producing mortar to construct the buildings. (Author's collection.)

By 1937, the King of Missions had again regained prominence within the chain of Spanish missions. Fr. Antonio Peyri was the last padre before Mexican secular laws, and he left an indelible impression by spending 34 years constructing the mission and overseeing its growth. He expanded several sub-mission properties towards other regions, including the asistencia Rancho Margarita y las Flores, an original Alta California rancho with rebuilt adobe brick quarters, chapel, and pasturelands between Mission San Luis Rey de Francia and Mission San Juan Capistrano.

Mission San Luis Rey de Francia received extensive renovations to the church beginning in 1893, after 40 years of neglect, and was rededicated after Franciscans reoccupied the church. A copper-sheathed lantern, atop the center of the church roof and transepts, had replaced the original, but it collapsed and was again repaired.

The traditional Blessing of Animals honors Saint Francis, the patron saint of animals within the Catholic Church. With the arrival of autumn, a procession of dogs, cats, and farm animals is annually celebrated at the mission on October 4. In his ode to God's living things, Saint Francis had written, "All praise to you, Oh Lord, for all these brother and sister creatures." (Southwest Museum of the American Indian Collection.)

Mission San Luis Rey de Francia was returned to the Roman Catholic bishop of Los Angeles after the land patent was restored in a proclamation signed by President Lincoln on March 18, 1865, less than one month before his assassination. A sale of its title early in 1846 by the Mexican governor, Pio Pico, had brought $2,437 for the properties but was nullified in June after the Bear Flag Revolt. The capture of General Vallejo, head of the northern Mexican military, led the way for American troops' victory and California's statehood by 1850. (Author's collection.)

After 1890, Franciscan monks again came to Mission San Luis Rey de Francia to restore its buildings, a work continuing today to retrofit earthquake safety standards. The courtyard and gardens within the cloister had 32 original archways, scaled back to 12 after they were rebuilt. (Southwest Museum of the American Indian Collection.)

Mission San Luis Rey de Francia was designated a National Historic Landmark in 1970. The roof of the church had been removed again in 2012 for safety upgrades. In a vintage postcard, the largest of all California missions gracefully frames the massive Moorish-style fountain. (Author's collection.)

Mission San Luis Rey de Francia was briefly the home of Franciscan refugees from Zacatecas, Mexico, seeking political asylum. In 1892, about 20 friars and novitiates migrated to inhabit Mission San Luis Rey de Francia as the first residents in 46 years since the death of Fray Jose Maria Zalvidea. New quarters would be set up for restoration work to begin. (Southwest Museum of the American Indian Collection.)

Fr. Joseph Jeremiah O'Keefe was stationed at Mission Santa Barbara nearly 25 years, spending 19 years rebuilding Mission San Luis Rey de Francia. He found that the church dome had collapsed and covered the floor with three feet of debris; raising nearly $50,000, he meticulously repaired the mission church, including minute details. In 1937, restorations were completed by skilled artisan Emmerich Piebel as part of the effort to preserve California's landmarks during the New Deal. (Southwest Museum of the American Indian Collection.)

Luiseño Mission Indians had lived for many generations near Mission San Luis de Francia. In 1832, a neophyte, Pablo Tac, left the mission with Fr. Antonio Peyri, the mission's builder, after deciding to avoid secularization policies. Tac later traveled to Rome, continuing his studies and writing several important pieces, including *The Conversion of the San Luiseños of Alta California* and *Indian Life and Customs at Mission San Luis Rey: A Record of California Mission Life*, as well as an important dictionary translating his native language to Spanish and Latin. (Southwest Museum of the American Indian Collection.)

The staircase to Fr. Antonio Peyri's private garden and courtyard leads from the private chapel at the side of the mission building. Many photographs were used to bring the mission back to authenticity. (Southwest Museum of the American Indian Collection.)

The eastern view from Mission San Luis Rey de Francia looks towards the foothills of Palomar Mountain. The mission sits within a rural part of San Diego's north county. The picturesque wooden cupola centered over the church nave allows light to enter. It is unique in design and materials among the California missions.

Mission San Luis Rey de Francia is pictured as it appeared during first restorations around 1895. The old mission had lost many buildings, outlined by arched porticos that were still standing. (Southwest Museum of the American Indian Collection.)

Fr. Joseph Jeremiah O'Keefe was born in County Cork, Ireland. He would spend 25 years as a missionary at Mission Santa Barbara, the only remaining California mission continuously under Franciscan administration. Solely responsible for raising initial support for restoring Mission San Luis Rey de Francia, his efforts were based on the original plans for the church. His work spanned 19 years, ending in 1912. (Southwest Museum of the American Indian Collection.)

The cloth habits of the Franciscan order became uniformly dark brown after 1897, when Pope Leo XIII prescribed the idea. Before then, many friars of the order had chosen red, blues, and black, among other colors. (Southwest Museum of the American Indian Collection.)

Mission San Luis Rey de Francia celebrates the day of its patron, Saint Antony de Padua, on the Feast of Saint Francis of Assisi in October. The mission church is a special setting for many musical concerts held throughout the year. (Escondido Public Library, Pioneer Room.)

The single bell tower of Mission San Luis de Francia rises above the cemetery at the eastern side of the church, photographed at the turn of the century. In 1843, Gov. Manuel Micheltorena restored Mission San Luis Rey to Franciscan control with about 400 faithful still remaining there. Impoverished conditions at the mission complex gave way to vandalism and resulted in the loss of entire buildings, leaving the dome and roof of the church near collapse. (Southwest Museum of the American Indian Collection.)

The main altar was surrounded by the massive Mission San Luis Rey de Francia church, completed by 1810 by Fr. Antonio Peyri, and included the padres' quarters, shops, granary, and storehouses. This early photograph of the main mission altar was made after long neglect. (Escondido Public Library, Pioneer Room.)

The cemetery, located behind the arched wall, and the entrance and cornice continue a complex balance of architecture from Moorish, Mexican, and Spanish heritage. Bright colors were made from native plants and clay and used to highlight decorative edges of all the buildings. The walls were strengthened with *ladrillo*, applied fired tile or brick veneering that had been used to protect the surfaces, then washed with limestone.

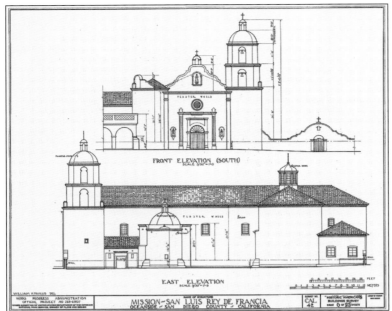

Drawings for Mission San Luis Rey de Francia were a crucial key to its accurate restorations. The first church was dedicated in 1802, the foundations of the present church were begun in 1811, and the mission was completed in 1815. By 1829, a domed roof had been finished, and the interior walls and ceiling were decorated by the native Indians.

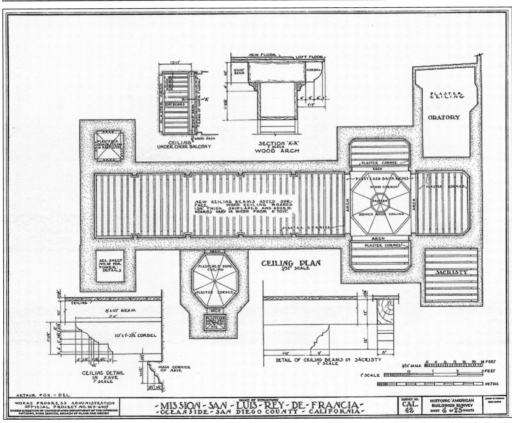

The King of the Missions was founded in 1797 by Fr. Fermín Francisco de Lasuén and built by Fr. Antonio Peyri in 1811. It was the largest building in California until the mid-1800s, representing more than any other mission in California a time of prosperity and expansion.

Three

THE HEADWATERS OF RIO DEL SAN LUIS REY
MISSION SAN ANTONIO DE PALA

The Mission San Antonio de Pala *capilla* was founded on October 4, 1815, by Fr. Antonio Peyri as a branch of Mission San Luis Rey de Francia. An asistencia, the substation had been built for the Pala tribe at their traditional home near the headwaters of the San Luis Rey River at the base of Palomar Mountain. The bell tower was a copy of an old church in Juarez, Mexico. Rising 50 feet above the cemetery, it has become an iconic landmark from the earliest days of California's missions. (Author's collection.)

A small cactus at the foot of the cross above the bell tower reflects Fr. Antonio Peyri's saga of prickly pear conquering the wilderness. By the turn of the century, the mission church had been reconstructed as an exact duplicate using original and modern materials and employing the same design and measurements. The adobe brick walls of the cemetery were in partial ruin after years of secularized laws left the mission abandoned. The tower's foundation was destroyed in 1916 from a winter of heavy rains and was later reconstructed. This photograph was taken about 1937. (Author's collection.)

Mission San Antonio de Pala began as the asistencia of Mission San Luis Rey de Francia and became a full mission central to many chapels in and around the great San Luis Rey River Valley. The mission had a priest in residence, and a traveling ministry by visiting padres was made since the founding. The mission served the outlying estancias at Rincon Chapel, La Jolla Chapel, Cahuilla Chapel, Santa Rosa Chapel, Temecula Chapel, Pichana Chapel, and Pauma Chapel nearby. San Margarita y las Flores, an asistencia, had fallen to ruin 35 years after an elaborate group of adobe buildings was built in 1823 by Fr. Antonio Peyri between Mission San Juan Capistrano and Oceanside. (Author's collection.)

Long before many mission restorations at the turn of the century, the original Mission San Antonio de Pala campanile stood as a lasting symbol. Undermined by floods during the winter of 1916, the tower completely toppled in heavy rains. This dramatic picture from the early era previous to the rebuilding of the iconic 50-foot tower is depicted in a vintage Detroit Publishing Co. postcard. Today, the Pala Indian Reservation contains approximately 12,000 acres in north San Diego County. (Author's collection.)

Mission San Antonio de Pala had been supervised by the Verona Fathers (Sons of the Sacred Heart) since 1948. The postcard pictured had been available during the 1960s to visitors at the mission just a short distance from San Diego's downtown. (Author's collection.)

Fr. Januarius Carillo began restorations of the surrounding quadrangle in 1954. By May 1955, one wing of the restoration was dedicated as the padre's residence. In 1958, new beams were brought to restore the roofing structure. The remaining artifacts displayed at the mission museum are open to public view. The figures, Our Lady of Lourdes and a full-sized crucifixion, were brought from Spain and Italy, respectively, for the courtyard garden. (Author's collection.)

San Antonio de Pala has continued operating since the founding days, with visiting pastors ministering to the faithful throughout the transition to secularization. Verona Fathers have occupied the mission since 1948, maintaining a long tradition of continuous service. (Southwest Museum of the American Indian Collection.)

After an earthquake in 1899, the tower's footing had partially given way, and the mission's chapel was also damaged, with the roof over the sanctuary collapsing. After 1902, Charles Fletcher Lummis, head of the Landmarks Club, had a defined purpose, "to conserve the Missions and other historic landmarks of Southern California," and rescued the property from absolute ruin. (Southwest Museum of the American Indian Collection.)

The California Landmarks Club, headed by Charles F. Lummis, first investigated the state of the mission premises in 1901 and noted disrepair of walls and adobe piers carrying the corridor roof. Under his guidance, restorations of the chapel and adjoining apartments began by roofing and reframing the living quarters with cedar logs from Mount Palomar, with rough pine furring supporting the roofing tiles. Included in the original materials used in the restoration were nine-inch-square, two-inch-thick floor tiles. At the front gate, nearly two centuries later, Mission San Antonio de Pala looks stunningly authentic today. (Author's collection.)

The mission chapel, long and narrow, drew its attendees towards the soft luminescence of the sanctuary, with colorful decorative frescos and statuary often made by mission Indians. The statue on the left is of Saint Louis IX, king of France, who lived from 1215 to 1270. (Southwest Museum of the American Indian Collection.)

By the turn of the century, Mission San Antonio de Pala's sanctuary displayed authentic designs, decorative paintings, and religious statuary from many restorations made by the Landmarks Club. The chapel remained surrounded by the ruins of its early adobe buildings from the original quadrangle, which was restored much later. (Southwest Museum of the American Indian Collection.)

After the Landmarks Club restoration of 1903, the mission received newly evicted Cupeños, a tribe from nearby Warner Springs, after a decision made by the US Supreme Court to assimilate the tribe with Pala Indians at the reservation. The asistencia had started with a granary built in 1810 by Fr. Antonio Peyri, the architect and builder of San Luis Rey de Francia. The chapel was completed by 1816. Milled Oregon lumber replaced the original roofing beams in 1902–1903, and the floor of the chancel was replaced with cement, as well as the floor of the arcade at front. All the doors, sash, shutters, and frames were replaced with local pine and whitewashed. Original window openings, shuttered when needed, were restored. Older photographs were a key to determining the condition and authenticity of the interiors by historians and archeologists, but much of the original artistry was thought to be lost when redone during the first restoration period. It appears that up to 25 authentic frescos within the interior of the chapel were covered with whitewash. During a subsequent period, the Indian decorations had been faithfully restored with new colors and additional designs.

A tribe called the Cupeños had been living in solitude until 1810, encountering little disturbance from Spanish settlers. In later times, their land became a popular destination known for its healthy sulfur springs. During a short period of revolt after demanding rights, the native residents fully rebelled against newcomers to their ancestral home. This was ended decisively by the US Supreme Court in 1901, and the Cupeños were ordered to leave behind their homelands to reside 40 miles away at the Pala reservation.

The familiar peal of mission bells brought travelers along El Camino Real to the eastern Mission San Antonio de Pala, which today remains a historic California mission destination. With many sub-missions established, Mission San Antonio de Pala, and its neighboring asistencia, Mission Santa Ysabel, in Julian, served the diverse communities of the San Diego region. The early friars had been inspired to lead discovery trails and reach the surrounding territories where many native inhabitants lived.

This iconic photograph from 1911 of Mission San Antonio de Pala was taken by Lewis C. Ryan. The Escondido resident, with his wife Frances, had researched the local history and the historical relationships between the missions. The influences of Mission San Diego de Alcalá and the grandest, Mission San Luis Rey de Francia, were unavoidable, and they attracted generations of friendly and cooperative indigenous people into mission communities. (Escondido Public Library, Pioneer Room.)

A vintage print from the 1930s was taken by its owner at the front of the historic Mission San Antonio de Pala, perhaps on a Sunday visit. A new period of heightened interest in California's early buildings was spurred by new restorations that increased public visitation by automobile to the mission, which was a short drive from San Diego's downtown. (Author's collection.)

A vintage Tin Lizzy parked at the padre's quarters was the most common mode of transportation at Mission San Antonio de Pala around 1928, as distances had become shortened to an hour's drive from the hub of the growing city of San Diego.

The Pala store was run by community natives and occupied part of the mission quadrangle of buildings, once in ruins from years of weathering. The mission complex had been restored during the 1950s, and the store moved to a newer building across the main street.

The Pauma Indians lived near the headwaters of rich rivers, a valuable resource for agriculture and pastureland. Nearby, Mission San Luis Rey de Francia had completed construction of an immense quadrangle in 1798, and Father Peyri decided to expand eastward, where he located the new asistencia chapel in 1815 near an existing adobe granary. It would become a center serving more than 1,000 Pala and Pauma Indians in the early years. The Pauma and Yuima reservation encompases nearly 6,000 acres near the base of Mt. Palomar. The reservation was established in 1872 and adjoins the Pala Indian reservation. Many small estancia chapels were constructed and visited by padres in rural areas of San Diego County.

Restorations of 1920 brought the repairs at the mission to near completion after nearly a century of neglect to the adobe buildings. The original chapel, two large granaries, a large apartment for the boys and young men, and another for girls and single women were all built of adobe brick with tile roofing. The original quadrangle of the mission had been completed between 1816 and 1818 and remained in ruins until 1958.

An old adobe is symbolic of the past at the Pala reservation and stood directly behind Mission San Antonio de Pala. Mission culture had increased to great prosperity, and the Franciscans brought irrigation to grow wheat, corn, beans, and garbanzos before the secular laws of 1823. This photograph from around 1930 aptly represents the passing of the old missions and ranchos of California into a modern era.

The entrance to Mission San Antonio de Pala is depicted around 1930, after many years of restorations. New beams from Mount Palomar had replaced the roof support. Each bell is original to the mission of 1815. The upper bell's inscription reads, "Holy Mary Pray For Us." The entire mission complex was rededicated after full restoration in 1959 by the bishop of San Diego, Rev. Charles F. Buddy.

Chief Juan Owlingish, a Cupeño Indian, is pictured at Mission San Antonio de Pala. His entire tribe was displaced from their homeland by federal order in 1901. (Southwest Museum of the American Indian Collection.)

The church interior had been lengthened in 1818, measuring 144 feet by 27 feet, and it was restored by 1920, after the original chapel had deteriorated. A granite altar rebuilt by a mission Indian replaced the original. (Southwest Museum of the American Indian Collection.)

Mission San Antonio de Pala's rectory entrance is shown in this photograph. The mission is in the care of Camboni Missionaries, an order begun in 1867 by Bishop Daniel Camboni, a great missionary of Africa. The order of missionaries is also called the Verona Fathers and Sisters and occupied the mission beginning in 1948. (Southwest Museum of the American Indian Collection.)

Thomas J. Conaty, bishop of Monterey–Los Angeles, visits the annual Feast of Corpus Christi surrounded by native parishioners. The iconic campanile is the original, pictured prior to the 1916 floods that toppled it. (Southwest Museum of the American Indian Collection.)

A postcard view shows the old campanario at the Mission San Antonio de Pala during the ceremony of the Feast of Corpus Christi, commemorating the institution of the Holy Eucharist in the church and also the first day of the mission's annual fiesta. The date varies according to Easter and Pentecostal Sundays; it is celebrated on the Thursday after Trinity Sunday, which is the week after Pentecost Sunday. The altar boys dress in red and white vestments and carry torches, performing solemn ceremonies. (Author's collection.)

Prior to 1915, Bishop Thomas J. Conaty (center, in gate) had been involved with the restoration projects within the Monterey–Los Angeles Diocese. He and the congregation of Mission San Antonio de Pala were supported by restoration projects headed by local citizens of the regional school system. The community would rejoice on the Feast of Corpus Christi, a celebratory gathering lasting over weeks. (Southwest Museum of the American Indian Collection.)

A revered statue of Saint Anthony, patron saint of the Mission San Antonio de Pala, is among the precious artifacts in the chapel. Although many liturgical items were imported, decorative designs and woodcarvings were created by early parishioners, painted with the use of earth-toned colors made from clay and natural colorants, and meticulously restored. (Southwest Museum of the American Indian Collection.)

The annual Mass of the Feast of Corpus Christi is traditionally celebrated before the mission's Fiesta Days, which last several weeks and were begun by the first padres at the mission. It includes an Indian choir and an early-style pit barbeque and features the sounds of music with primitive Indian dances. Traditionally, the young girls dressed in white and scattered flowers in the path of the procession. (Southwest Museum of the American Indian Collection.)

The lower, larger bell has inscriptions in Latin and Spanish: "Our Patron Saint Francis of Assisi. Saint Louis the King. Saint Clara Culalia Our Light Cervantes Made Us." (Southwest Museum of the American Indian Collection.)

In 1948, the Verona Fathers (Sons of the Sacred Heart) succeeded the Franciscans at Mission San Antonio de Pala. By 1913, the US Congress had ratified an allotment of land for the reservation, and new housing was built around the mission. In 1954, the San Diego Diocese gave the blessing of the church to restore the entire quadrangle complex. (Southwest Museum of the American Indian Collection.)

The original Mission San Antonio de Pala survived its state of dilapidation. On Christmas Day, 1899, an earthquake rumbled through the entire Pala Valley, destroying the chapel roof, and the roof tiles fell into the church floor. In tragic ruins, the Landmarks Club and its president, Charles F. Lummis, purchased the quadrangle, rescued the buildings, and first partially repaired the main chapel and two adjoining rooms.

Today, the Mission San Antonio de Pala chapel is fully repaired. With the work of the Pala Indian tribe, adobe bricks cast by the thousands were created for the modern restorations. The cultural art displayed on the north wall has a few of the symbols preserved from their belief systems over the past 200 years. The cultural blending between the padres and the Indians is evident from a long-lasting bond into modern times. (Southwest Museum of the American Indian Collection.)

Mission San Antonio de Pala's roof and adobe structure had greatly decayed by the beginning of the 20th century. The Pala region was famous for its semiprecious gems lepidolite, tourmaline, kunzite, and quartz crystals. (Southwest Museum of the American Indian Collection.)

In 1877, William Veal received a patent for the lands including Mission San Antonio de Pala, and by 1833, he had been persuaded by his wife, a devout Catholic, to return the lands to the Pala mission Indians and the Catholic Church. Charles F. Lummis, leader of the Landmarks Club of Southern California, purchased the remainder of the main quadrangle and ruins and started restorations of the chapel in 1902. (Southwest Museum of the American Indian Collection.)

Mission San Antonio de Pala attracted the attention of early restorers, and by the turn of the century, it led the path for many other California Mission restorations. Bringing back to life the legendary buildings and iconic designs greatly appealed to the public interest. A nearby school created its own project to help the restoration. (Author's collection.)

The Pauma chapel was established on companion lands neighboring the Pala reservation. San Diego had the most distinct native tribal groups and languages in all the territories of Alta California. Many regional San Diego tribes were moved or decimated through legal actions, but remained cherished icons of past generations of native Californians, still being used today.

This artful image portrays a serene view of the Old Mission San Antonio de Pala and its iconic campanario rising over the valley. Standing at the foot of the mission graveyard and rising 50 feet above the valley, the bell tower still holds the original mission bells of 1816. (Author's collection.)

The roof tiles original to the 1816 mission were spread throughout the district over time and now show up on various buildings. Restorations included using many reclaimed tiles. The heavy buttressed back wall of the church is plastered and whitewashed, common to adobe construction.

In a picturesque photograph by Charles F. Lummis, a well-known mission restorer, the freestanding campanile became an iconic image admired for its authenticity. Although the mission quadrangle had fallen into rubble, Lummis rescued the ruined church and several adjacent quarters. (Southwest Museum of the American Indian Collection.)

The original bell tower survived nearly a century until the winter of 1915–1916, when storms and unrelenting rains undermined the foundation of the venerable structure until it fell. A duplicate tower was reconstructed, maintaining the original shape and measurements. (Southwest Museum of the American Indian Collection.)

Edward S. Curtis (1868–1952) was a legendary photographer. He created many iconic portraits of Native Americans documenting their vanishing tribalism. These became timeless images of California's original residents. The photographs often revealed personalities, traits, and skills and were often greatly enhanced in their composition through poses, intricate handmade items, and background dwellings. This child subject was from the eastern Cahuilla tribe, a distant rancho from the missionary days.

This photograph was taken by Edward S. Curtis at the eastern edge of the Mohave Desert on the trail to the Mission San Antonio de Pala region. His photographs depicted the beauty of the era and documented vanishing images of America, native lifestyles, and their conditions. All native populations had been affected by the transition from the earliest mission period to succeeding Mexican and American generations in California. Indigenous people were willing to coexist with California's settlements, an evolution Curtis recognized and memorialized with photography.

Maria Antonia, a basket maker at Pala, works outside a thatched dwelling of tule reeds near San Diego in 1914. Within the mission culture, local natives had been called Diegueños and were associated with the nearby Mission San Diego de Alcalá, spreading to the eastern desert's edge.

These useful and artful baskets were made by Southern California mission Indians. The photograph is by Edward S. Curtis.

Cinon Mataweer, a Pala Indian, stands wearing feathers about his waist and a headdress in front of his adobe structure near San Diego in 1914.

An adobe estancia was built at Warner Springs, near an important water source discovered by the friars in an area once home to the Cupeños. The entire tribe had been deported to the Pala reservation in May 1903. The eviction was ordered by the United States to allow ancestral Indian lands to be resettled. (Author's collection.)

An asistencia founded by Fr. Antonio Peyri in 1823 at Rancho San Pedro was called Las Flores. The complex of adobes was an extension to Mission San Luis Rey de Francia halfway to Mission San Juan Capistrano. The buildings included a tiled adobe church, a hostel, and stables with corrals. Corn, wheat, and barley grains were raised. The chapel was abandoned after 35 years, and newer adobe buildings were constructed. They later were incorporated as part of the Camp Pendleton Marine Corps base. The original mission footprint is located behind a present-day Boy Scout area inside the base. (Both, Southwest Museum of the American Indian Collection.)

This fine example of an adobe brick house near San Diego's San Pasqual Valley could tolerate the drier, cooler inland climate. It was covered with thatched roofing, had opposing fireplaces, and was constructed to accommodate colder weather at a higher elevation. The Diegueño Indians who lived here eventually were relocated to Pala, including Felicita, a witness as a young girl to the momentous upheaval of the Mexican-American War and the early mission culture.

Boley Morales and Felicita were life-long companions into an unknown old age, and both were considered centenarians by 1915. Felicita's legend endures as the Indian princess baptized by the early missionaries in San Diego. A survivor of the Battle of San Pasqual during the Mexican-American War, her name remains at the central Escondido park to memorialize native history in the area. (Escondido Public Library, Pioneer Room.)

Felicita, a baptized Diegueño Indian, witnessed the Battle of San Pasqual of 1846. She was a child of the chief, Pontho, who became a legend of Escondido. Her story was the subject of a historic Escondido play and pageant that depicted her romantically with an American soldier after the Battle of San Pasqual. The natives were thought to be fierce aborigines in the eastern foothills, but in truth, they peacefully roamed the hills and forests gathering acorns and seeds for food. The stylized pageant included actors Ben Sherman and Mildred Vorhees between 1927 and 1932. A modern production revived the play. (Escondido Public Library, Pioneer Room.)

San Pasqual Battlefield State Historic Park, outside of Escondido, was the scene of fierce fighting between American soldiers led by Gen. Stephen Kearny and the famous scout Kit Carson against the Californios in the Mexican-American War. The battle ended questionably, with each side suffering severe losses, while General Kearny held Mule Hill. The battle was thought to have helped bring California further under control of the United States. Carson walked shoeless in a desperate midnight run to find reinforcements at San Diego, saving the troops from complete disaster.

This Cupeño woman was photographed by Edward S. Curtis between 1905 and 1924. The tribe was originally part of the Warner Springs area and was ordered by the US Supreme Court into the Pala reservation after 1902 after a short rebellion. The Cupeño Indians considered it their own trail of tears, forced to move 40 miles away from their homeland.

Felicita La Chappa and Boley Morales, a life-long companion, lived in a small cabin until 1916, and Boley was said to have lived to 120. As a child, her name "Felicita" was chosen after a baptism given by the padres at Mission San Diego de Alcalá. (Escondido Public Library, Pioneer Room.)

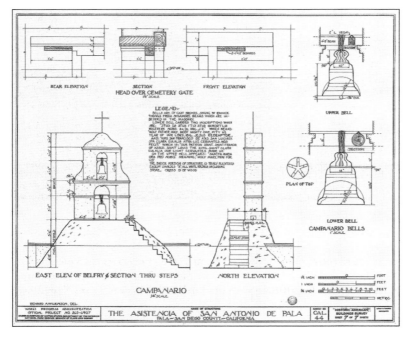

One of the earliest in California, the larger lower bell of the campanario carries inscriptions in Latin translating: "Holy Father, Most Mighty One, Have Mercy on Us, Year of Our Lord, 1816. Jesus Redemptor. Cervantes Made Us." The lower band is inscribed to honor "Our Seraphic Father, Francis of Assisi, San Luis King, Saint Clara, Saint Eulalia, Our Light."

Four

THE OUTLYING STATIONS
ASISTENCIA SANTA YSABEL

San Diego's earliest residents represented the most diversified of all California's native groups and spoke in many distinct tribal languages. Within the mission culture, they had been called Diegueños, and they were associated with the Mission San Diego de Alcalá, spreading to the eastern desert edge where a single outpost, named Mission Santa Ysabel, today rests in a picturesque foothill valley at 3,000 feet above the Black Canyon Ravine, pictured here. The mission name honored Saint Elizabeth, a Franciscan lay affiliate who died in 1336. Mission Santa Ysabel was founded by Fr. Fernando Martín on September 20, 1818, and was referred to as the "Church in the Desert."

Southern California indigenous people were related historically to two broad groupings, Shoshonean and Yuman. San Diego Indians are mostly related to Shoshonean tribes and were called Kumeyaay. The Cahuilla, like the woman pictured here, occupied the southern Mojave Desert at the turn of the century. Their name in their own language is Iviatim, and Ivia, their language, was traditionally spoken 50 miles inland and 50 miles northeast of the modern-day US–Mexico border. The tribe lived within the foothills of Mount Palomar and the San Bernadino Mountains. Today, Luiseño and Pala are names applied to many natives near Mission San Luis Rey de Francia. Others included the Morongo Band of Cahuilla Mission Indians, Los Coyotes Band of Cahuilla, and the Pauma and Cupeño Indians. This Edward S. Curtis photograph is from 1926.

This photograph by Edward S. Curtis documents the pure life of the desert Indians who had remained. Each tribe was influenced by the mission estancias extending eastward. Franciscan fathers noted how advanced native cultures used tools of stone and were of peaceful disposition. They wore few clothes except in colder weather. Similar to other indigenous people of California, they were seed and acorn gatherers who used a variety of baskets for harvests and stone pestles and mortars to grind staple foods.

Dedicated in 1924, St. John the Baptist Catholic Church was built on the site of old Mission Santa Ysabel. It is directed under the Sons of the Sacred Heart to serve the surrounding community. Luiseño and Diegueño people returned to their villages after secularization, which permitted the continuation of traditional native policies, leadership positions, and ritual systems. (Southwest Museum of the American Indian Collection.)

The beautiful interior of St. John the Baptist is pictured facing the altar. The church replaced the old Mission Santa Ysabel and connected the eastern trails of San Diego to the Church in the Desert. (Author's collection.)

The new church was built on the original site of Mission Santa Ysabel in honor of Fr. Edmond La Pointe, a Canada-born missionary serving the mountainous area for 29 years. (Escondido Public Library, Pioneer Room.)

An Indian drawing depicts the early Mission Santa Ysabel, once a simple brushwood ramada. These traditional places of gathering for the faithful were served by visiting padres of the old Mission San Diego de Alcalá. (Southwest Museum of the American Indian Collection.)

The legend of the "Angel of the Lost Bells" is represented by this carving by Stephen Barardi commemorating the original Mission Santa Ysabel. The mission bells were among the earliest in California. Indian faithful bought two bells for the mission for six loads of grain and carried them back on burros. Only the clappers have been found, and they are now displayed in the museum at the church. The mystery of the lost bells still remains. (Escondido Public Library, Pioneer Room.)

The bells of Mission San Ysabel, pictured in 1902, remained near the mission site until 1926. They mysteriously disappeared, leaving unsolved the reason they were confiscated, depriving the locals of the traditional peals. The original bells were purchased by Indians, and were cast in 1723 and 1767. (Southwest Museum of the American Indian Collection.)

A small chapel was built at the site of Mission Santa Ysabel to provide a temporary turn-of-the-century church near the old mission bells on the site of old Mission Santa Ysabel. Erosion had eaten away the various buildings and left the chapel in ruins, and all of the original adobe houses had vanished. Brush and mud ramadas temporarily served as a church and were usually propped against a remaining original adobe wall. Two bells, bought by the Indians for six burro loads of barley, hung in a frame and remained the only artifacts of the original chapel for decades.

The renowned photographer Edward S. Curtis recorded the lives of ancestral indigenous people at the beginning of the 20th century. The turmoil of the Mexican-American War ended the Mexican period of secularization laws and led to the abandonment of many mission colonies, dispersing mission Indians. Mission San Diego de Alcalá had begun with a large mission settlement and asistencia Mission Santa Ysabel, with many smaller estancias at neighboring ranchos. They are among the first settlements in California.

An elegant entrance flanked by mission bells and distinctive columns leads to the asistencia of Mission San Diego de Alcalá, the outpost of Mission Santa Ysabel. In 1818, the mission was erected in a remote area at a 3,000-foot elevation east of San Diego near the old mining town of Julian. All original buildings disintegrated, and in 1924, the Church of St. John the Baptist was built as a permanent mission chapel. (Escondido Public Library, Pioneer Room.)

Padre Fernando Martín blessed the spot for the new capilla at Cañada de Santa Ysabel on September 20, 1818. Padre Vincent Sarría was granted permission in February 2, 1819, to erect a permanent church. The new church was completed by 1822. After 1846, the original buildings had fallen into ruin.

Mission Santa Ysabel's graveyard has served generations, with thousands of mission Indians buried at the site. (Southwest Museum of the American Indian Collection.)

An early Native American weaving is displayed at Mission Santa Ysabel, the design made by mission Indians. The influences of Christian iconography are visible in the weaving. The remote mission is located on the trail to the Mohave Desert; it was established as an asistencia of California's first mission, San Diego de Alcalá.

Five

MISSIONS PAST AND PRESENT
TOURING EL CAMINO REAL

This 1949 newspaper photograph shows San Diego's Presidio Hill, site of the initial Alta California encampment of 1769 and first location of the Mission San Diego Alcalá. In 1774, the original mission was relocated about six miles to the banks of the San Diego River and its new adobe church was rededicated in 1813. All California missions are open to the public and are restored to their early luster after many years of research and careful reconstruction. Popular sightseeing adventures and bus tours include the Serra Museum, a familiar sight in San Diego near Old Town and home of the San Diego History Center, designed by architect William Templeton Johnson in 1928. (Author's collection.)

Above, the view atop Presidio Hill from Alta California's first settlement overlooks today's San Diego and is the location of the San Diego History Center's Serra Museum. To the far right are the locations of the first chapel site and the cross raised by Fr. Junípero Serra in 1769. Father Serra moved the mission to a new location in 1774, and a new adobe mission was completed in 1813 and restored in 1931. At left, the Serra Museum is a monument to California's heritage. From here, missionary pathfinders ventured north along El Camino Real, successfully settling the original 21 Spanish missions over the next 54 years. (Both, author's collection.)

Founded in San Diego by Father Serra in 1769, California's founding mission, Mission San Diego de Alcalá, was moved to its present location in 1774. Mission Basilica San Diego de Alcalá is located today at 10818 San Diego Mission Road in San Diego and can be reached at 619-283-6338 or www.missionsandiego.com. (Author's collection.)

The second California mission, founded by Fr. Junípero Serra in 1770, was Mission San Carlos de Borromeo del Rio Carmelo. Carmel Mission Basilica is at 3080 Rio Road in Carmel and can be reached at 831-624-1271 or www.carmelmission.org. (Author's collection.)

California's third mission was founded by Fr. Junípero Serra in 1771. Mission San Antonio de Padua is located at the end of Mission Road in Jolon and can be reached at 831-385-4478 or www.missionsanantonio.net. (Author's collection.)

The fourth California mission was founded by Fathers Pedro Benito Cambón and Angel Somera in 1771. Mission San Gabriel Arcángel is at 428 S. Mission Drive in San Gabriel and can be reached at 626-457-3035 or www.sangabrielmissionchurch.org. (Author's collection.)

The fifth California mission, Mission San Luis Obispo de Tolosa, was founded by Fr. Junípero Serra in 1772. Today, the mission's quadrangle is bordered by Palm, Chorro, Monterey and Broad Streets and can be visited at 751 Palm Street in San Luis Obispo or reached at 805-781-8220 or www.missionsanluisobispo.org. (Author's collection.)

The sixth California mission was founded by Fr. Junípero Serra in 1776. Mission San Francisco de Asís and Mission Dolores Basilica are located at 3321 Sixteenth Street in San Francisco and can be reached at 415-621-8203 or www.missiondolores.org. (Author's collection.)

The seventh California mission was founded by Fr. Fermín de Lasuén in 1776. Mission San Juan Capistrano is at 26801 Ortega Highway in San Juan Capistrano and can be reached at 714-234-1300 or www.missionsjc.com. (Author's collection.)

The eighth California mission was founded by Fr. Junípero Serra in 1777. Mission Santa Clara de Asís is at 500 East El Camino Real in Santa Clara and can be reached at 408-554-4356 or www.scu.edu/visitors/mission. (Author's collection.)

The ninth California mission was founded by Fr. Junípero Serra in 1782. Mission San Buenaventura is at 225 East Main Street between South Ventura and North Palm Streets in Ventura and can be reached at 805-648-4496 or www.sanbuenaventuramission.org. (Author's collection.)

The 10th California mission, Mission Santa Bárbara, Virgen y Mártir, was founded by Fr. Fermín de Lasuén in 1786. Old Mission Santa Barbara is at 2201 Laguna Street in Santa Barbara and can be reached at 805-682-4713 or www.santabarbaramission.org. (Author's collection.)

The 11th California mission was founded by Fr. Fermín de Lasuén in 1787. Mission La Purísima Concepción de María Santísima is found in La Purisima Mission State Historic Park at 2295 Purisima Road in Lompoc and can be reached at 805-733-3713 or www.lapurisimamission.org. (Author's collection.)

The 12th California mission was founded by Fr. Fermín de Lasuén in 1791. Mission La Exaltacion de la Santa Cruz is in Santa Cruz Mission State Historic Park at 144 School Street in Santa Cruz and can be reached at 831-426-5686 or www.parks.ca.gov. (Author's collection.)

The 13th California mission was founded by Fr. Fermín de Lasuén in 1791. Mission Nuestra Señora del la Soledad is at 36641 Fort Romie Road in Soledad and can be reached at 831-678-2586 or www.cityofsoledad.com. (Author's collection.)

The 14th California mission was founded by Fr. Fermín de Lasuén in 1797. Old Mission San Jose is at 43300 Mission Boulevard at Washington Boulevard in Fremont and can be reached at 510-657-1797 or www.missionsanjose.org. (Author's collection.)

The 15th mission was founded by Fr. Fermín de Lasuén in 1797 and named for Saint John the Baptist. Old Mission San Juan Bautista is at 406 Second Street in San Juan Bautista and can be reached at 831.623.4528 or www.oldmissionsjb.org. (Author's collection.)

The 16th California mission was founded by Fr. Fermín de Lasuén in 1797. San Miguel, Arcángel is at 775 Mission Street in San Miguel and can be reached at 805-467-3256 or www.missionsanmiguel.org. (Author's collection.)

The 17th California mission was founded by Fr. Fermín de Lasuén in 1797. Mission San Fernando Rey de España is at 15151 San Fernando Mission Boulevard in Mission Hills and includes a historical museum with an archival center. It can be reached at 818-361-0186 or www.archivalcenter.org. (Author's collection.)

The 18th California mission was founded by Fr. Fermín de Lasuén in 1798. Mission San Luis Rey de Francia is at 4050 Mission Avenue in Oceanside and can be reached at 760-757-3651 or www.sanluisrey.org. (Author's collection.)

The 19th California mission was founded by Fr. Estévan Tápis in 1804 and was named for Saint Agnes. Old Mission Santa Inés is at 1760 Mission Drive in Solvang and can be reached at 805-688-4815 or www.missionsantaines.org. (Author's collection.)

The 20th California mission was founded by Fr. Vicente de Sarría in 1817, first as an asistencia. It was granted full mission status in 1822. Mission San Rafael Arcángel is at 1104 Fifth Avenue in San Rafael and can be reached at 415-454-8141 or www.saintraphael.com. (Author's collection.)

The 21st California mission was founded in 1823 by Fr. José Altamira and named for Saint Francis Solano, a missionary to the Peruvian Indians. Mission San Francisco Solano is the last Spanish mission in California and is part of Sonoma State Historic Park and is located at 20 East Spain Street in Sonoma. It can be reached at 707-938-1519 or www.parks.ca.gov. (Author's collection.)

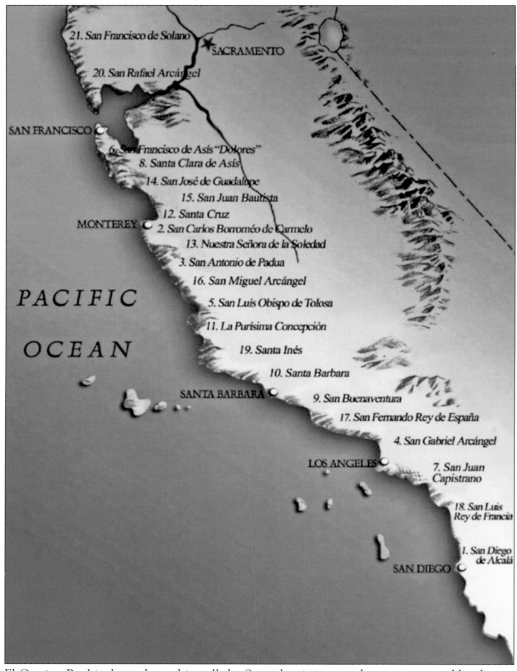

21. San Francisco de Solano
SACRAMENTO
20. San Rafael Arcángel

SAN FRANCISCO
6. San Francisco de Asís "Dolores"
8. Santa Clara de Asís
14. San José de Guadalupe
15. San Juan Bautista
12. Santa Cruz
MONTEREY
2. San Carlos Borroméo de Carmelo
13. Nuestra Señora de la Soledad
3. San Antonio de Padua
16. San Miguel Arcángel

PACIFIC
5. San Luis Obispo de Tolosa
11. La Purísima Concepción
19. Santa Inés

OCEAN
10. Santa Barbara
SANTA BARBARA
9. San Buenaventura
17. San Fernando Rey de España
4. San Gabriel Arcángel
LOS ANGELES
7. San Juan Capistrano
18. San Luis Rey de Francia
1. San Diego de Alcalá
SAN DIEGO

El Camino Real is the path reaching all the Spanish missions, with many separated by about a day's journey, forming a chain. The earliest trails between missions extended from Guatemala and Mexico over thousands of miles and were developed by missionaries coming to Baja and Alta California. Father Serra dreamed of mission colonies throughout Alta California, and Franciscan settlements grew to 21 monumental missions and several asistencia sub-missions and smaller estancia stations.

BIBLIOGRAPHY

Berger, John A. *The Franciscan Missions of California*. Garden City, NY: Doubleday & Co., 1948.

Carillo, Fr. J.M. *The Story of Mission San Antonio de Pala*. Balboa Island, CA: Pisano Press Inc., 1967.

Chapman, Charles E. *A History of California: The Spanish Period*. New York, NY: Macmillan, 1921.

Elder, Paul. *The Old Spanish Missions of California*. San Francisco, CA: Paul Elder and Co., 1913.

Gudde, Erwin G. *1000 Place Names*. Berkeley and Los Angeles, CA: UC Press, 1965.

Hoover, Mildred Brooke; Hero Eugene Reusch; and Ethel Grace Reusch. *Historic Spots in California*. Stanford, CA: Stanford University Press, 1953.

Kimbro, Edna E. and Julia G. Costello, with Tevvy Ball. *The Missions of California*. Los Angeles, CA: J. Paul Getty Museum, 2009.

Mornin, Edward and Lorna. *Saints of California*. Los Angeles, CA: J. Paul Getty Museum, 2009.

Ryan, Frances B. and Lewis C. *Yes Escondido, There Was a Felicita!* Self-published, 1980.

Wright, Ralph B. *California's Missions*. Los Angeles, CA: Sterling Press, 1950.

Discover Thousands of Local History Books
Featuring Millions of Vintage Images

Arcadia Publishing, the leading local history publisher in the United States, is committed to making history accessible and meaningful through publishing books that celebrate and preserve the heritage of America's people and places.

Find more books like this at
www.arcadiapublishing.com

Search for your hometown history, your old stomping grounds, and even your favorite sports team.